BLACK HOLES

Katie Parker

This edition first published in 2010 in the United States
of America by Marshall Cavendish Benchmark.

Marshall Cavendish Benchmark
99 White Plains Road
Tarrytown, NY 10591
www.marshallcavendish.us

All Internet addresses were available and accurate when this book went to press.

Library of Congress Cataloging-in-Publication Data
Parker, Katie, 1974–
Black holes / by Katie Parker.
p. cm. — (Big ideas in science)
Summary: "Provides comprehensive information on the history of black holes,
as well as the many types that exist"—Provided by publisher.
Includes bibliographical references and index.
ISBN 978-0-7614-4392-6
1. Black holes (Astronomy)—Juvenile literature. I. Title.
QB843.B55 P37 2010
523.8'875—dc22
2008055994

The photographs in this book are used by permission and through the courtesy of:
Cover: Neo Edmund/Shuttertock, T. A. Rector & B. A. Wolpa/NOAO
Half Title: ESA/Hubble
pp4-5: De Agostini Picture Library/Getty Images; p5(inset): James Steidl/Fotolia; p6: Photolibrary;
p7: The Gallery Collection/Corbis; p8: Bettmann/Corbis; p9: Michael Nicholson/Corbis;
p10: Michael Zysman; p12: Elizabeth Netterstrom/Alamy; p15: Jim Mills/Shutterstock;
p16tr: James Davis; Eye Ubiquitous/Corbis; p16bl: Photolibrary; pp18-19: Dreamstime;
pp20-21: iStockphoto; pp22-23: 123RF; p23(inset): Dreamstime; p26: Mary Evans Picture Library/
Photolibrary; p27: Hulton-Deutsch Collection/Corbis; p29: NASA; p31: Frans Lanting/Corbis;
p34: iStockphoto; p35: Dreamstime; p36: National Library of Medicine; p39: Tose/Dreamstime;
p41: Science Photo Library; p42(inset): iStockphoto; p44: Photolibrary.
Illustrations: Q2AMedia Art Bank

Created by Q2AMedia
Art Director: Sumit Charles
Editor: Denise Pangia
Series Editor: Penny Dowdy
Client Service Manager: Santosh Vasudevan
Project Manager: Shekhar Kapur
Designer: Prashant Kumar
Illustrators: Prachand Verma, Ajay Sharma,
Bibin Jose, Abhideep Jha, and Rajesh Das
Photo Research: Shreya Sharma

Printed in Malaysia

1 3 5 6 4 2

Contents

Infinite Mystery   4

Black Hole Basics   6

A Star Is Born   10

The Death of Stars   14

Type I: Stellar Black Holes   18

Deeper into Black Holes   22

Type II: Supermassive Monsters   26

The Search for the Invisible   30

Other Types of Black Holes   34

Time Dilation   38

Myths and Possibilities   42

Glossary   46

Find Out More   47

Index   48

Infinite Mystery

Which is deeper—a black hole or the mystery that surrounds a black hole? These holes in space are the greatest enigmas, or riddles, of the universe. The more we learn about them, the more questions we have. Perhaps that is why black holes appear so often in science-fiction books, movies, and even myths!

It seems that black holes interest everyone: scientists, screenwriters, novelists—and people just like you. These monsters have plagued the world's leading minds for centuries. They have captured the imaginations of thousands of people. Yet, we understand so little about them!

There is a lot of information out there about black holes, but much of it is false. Do you know the truth? Are they deep holes in space? Can anything escape their grasp? Do they swallow everything in their path? Are they invisible? And what about the movies that have been made about time traveling through a black hole? Surely, that's just a crazy idea—or is it?

The artist who drew this picture can only guess what a black hole looks like. No one has ever seen one.

Researchers are not sure what this image shows. It could be a blob of cosmic gas being sucked into a deadly black hole.

We hear that black holes act like starving monsters. They pull gases, planets, stars, and even light into a swirling death spiral. Are we safe from black holes? Or does a deadly menace sit at the center of our galaxy, waiting to swallow Earth?

Stop! It's important to separate fact from fiction. When you're finished reading about black holes, you'll have answers to many of your questions about one of the universe's most misunderstood **bodies**. In order to make sense of the answers, though, you must first understand the science behind the stories.

Since the 1700s, people have suspected that black holes existed. But no one has ever seen one in action. In fact, the first evidence was in 2001. A scientist named Joseph Dolan showed some photographs he had taken. He claimed that they showed a gaseous blob being sucked into a suspected black hole. Yet, even Dolan warned that the photos alone do not provide enough data for scientists to be sure of what they saw.

Black Hole Basics

Amazingly enough, early astronomers and physicists came close to predicting the existence of black holes.

Centuries ago scientists were focusing on questions whose answers seem like common sense to us now. In the late 1600s a scientist and mathematician named Sir Isaac Newton discovered gravity. A legend says that he was hit in the head by a falling apple and wondered, why did the apple fall down? Why not up?

He theorized that the apple fell to earth because of mass and gravity. Mass is the amount of matter an object contains. Gravity is the force that pulls one object toward another. An object with greater mass has a stronger gravitational pull than one with less mass.

What does all this have to do with Newton's apple? Earth is much more massive than an apple. So the apple is pulled toward Earth when it falls. Earth is also more massive than the Moon. That's why the Moon orbits, or circles, Earth rather than traveling out into space. Similarly, the Sun is more massive than any of the planets. The Sun's gravitational pull keeps the planets orbiting around it.

A black hole's mass creates a powerful force that causes nearby objects to orbit around it. Sometimes these objects are pulled into what seems like an abyss, or bottomless hole.

In order to break out of its orbit, an object must reach a speed known as escape velocity. For example, to escape Earth's gravitational pull, a rocket must travel about 25,000 miles (40,234 kilometers) per hour! Black holes have tremendous mass. Nothing can reach the escape velocity required to break away!

Newton never imagined black holes existed. Yet, scientists have used his theories to explain black holes and why they are so powerful. In the 1700s, an English scientist named John Michell used Newton's ideas to figure out the movement of stars and other bodies. He suggested that if an object in space were supermassive, nothing could escape its gravitational force. He wondered if such objects existed.

A rocket can escape Earth's gravitational force. First, it must reach a speed known as escape velocity.

The bodies in our solar system have different masses. That means some have a stronger gravitational field than others. The stronger the field is, the higher the escape velocity must be. Jupiter is the largest planet and has the most mass. It has an escape velocity of about 134,708 miles per hour (216,792 km/h)! Mercury is the least massive planet and has the lowest escape velocity: about 9,506 miles per hour (15,298 km/h). Earth is more massive than Mercury. It has an escape velocity of 25,000 miles per hour (40,234 km/h). Compare that to the speed of large passenger planes. They have an average speed of only about 290 miles per hour (467 km/h)!

Michell also wondered about the effect such an object would have on light. Light travels at about 186,000 miles (300,000 km) per second. Michell imagined black holes had an escape velocity even faster than the speed of light. If that were true, then black holes would suck in light. They would be invisible!

A French scientist named Pierre-Simon Laplace agreed. He said, "It is possible that the largest **luminous** bodies of the universe may be invisible." No one thought much about this possibility for almost two hundred years. Then, Albert Einstein came along. He published his **General Theory of Relativity** and his **Special Theory of Relativity**.

In his theories, Einstein described space and time as being part of the same fabric. He called this fabric space-time. Unlike other scientists, Einstein thought gravity was a property of space-time, which meant that it could change. He explained that the more massive an object was, the stronger its gravitational pull would be. According to Einstein, the mass of an object causes space-time to stretch and warp, creating a dip in space-time called a gravity well. A less-massive object would be pulled into the well. Think of space-time as a mattress and a bowling ball as a massive object. The bowling ball will create a dip in the mattress similar to a gravity well. If you put a baseball (a less-massive object) on the mattress, too, it will roll toward the bowling ball and into the gravity well.

Einstein's theories of relativity taught us even more about the relationship between gravity and mass.

Einstein also stated that mass and energy were forms of the same thing. As such, energy could also warp space-time. The warping would only be noticeable if something were moving at an extremely high speed. Nearly one hundred years later, research still supports these theories.

Einstein called the speed of light the universal speed limit. Nothing else could reach that speed. Yet, even he believed in invisible black holes. Like Michell, he theorized that if a body were massive enough, its escape velocity could be faster than the speed of light. A black hole is such a body. It is so massive that its escape velocity is more than 186,000 miles (300,000 km) per second. Einstein agreed that not even light could escape the gravity well caused by a massive black hole.

Black holes were not named until 1967, when American physicist John Wheeler came up with the term. The name *black hole* was intriguing, so the public became very interested in them. Prior to their naming, only scientists were interested in the possibility of black holes. Wheeler also theorized that black holes came from stars. He was right!

According to the General Theory of Relativity, an object's mass causes space-time to curve around it. This creates a gravity well. The more massive an object is, the deeper its gravity well. This diagram shows that Jupiter stretches space-time more than Earth, which stretches it more than Mars.

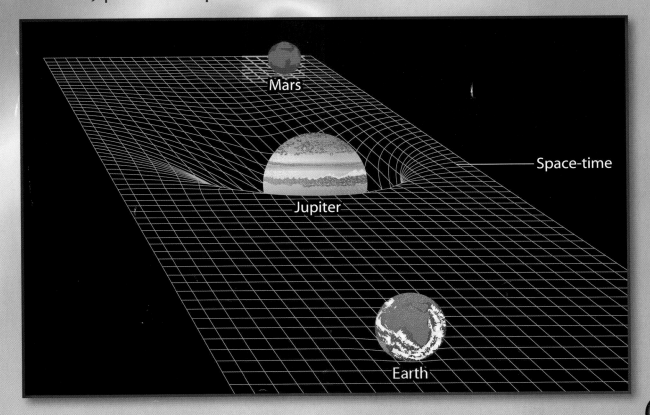

A Star Is Born

Many black holes start out as stars. You've seen stars. Are they really glowing, five-pointed objects? No. They are not even solid. Stars are masses of gases held together by their own gravity.

Floating dust and atoms of gas fill outer space. Over millions of years, they may form a cloud called a stellar nebula. As the stellar nebula increases in mass, its gravity well deepens. More and more dust and gases are pulled into the center of the nebula. This process is called accretion. The stellar nebula grows, and the center of its gravity well becomes very dense. At this point, the center of the gravity well is called a protostar, which is the earliest stage of a star. The protostar heats up for millions of years.

From Earth, we see stars of many different colors. The color of a star indicates its surface temperature.

Remember that gases and dust are always falling into the gravity well. The constant stream of debris creates high pressure in the protostar. The pressure increases the heat, which causes atoms to move faster and bump into each other. When the core gets hot enough, hydrogen atoms crash into each other at such high speeds that they create a fusion reaction. A fusion reaction takes place when the nuclei (plural of *nucleus*, which is the center of an atom) of two atoms join together. The very first fusion reaction results in a bright, hot burst of light within the stellar nebula. This is the birth of a star.

Additional fusion reactions provide the star with much-needed fuel. They also continue to release energy as heat and light, which makes the star glow. For the rest of the star's life, fusion reactions will make it shine.

A stellar nebula can be quite beautiful. As more gas and dust are pulled into the center, a protostar will form.

Not every stellar nebula becomes a star. In order for fusion reactions to occur, the core of the star must be hot and massive enough. Some stellar nebulae come together in a protostar, but they never gain enough mass or heat for fusion reactions to occur. Scientists call these failed stars brown dwarfs.

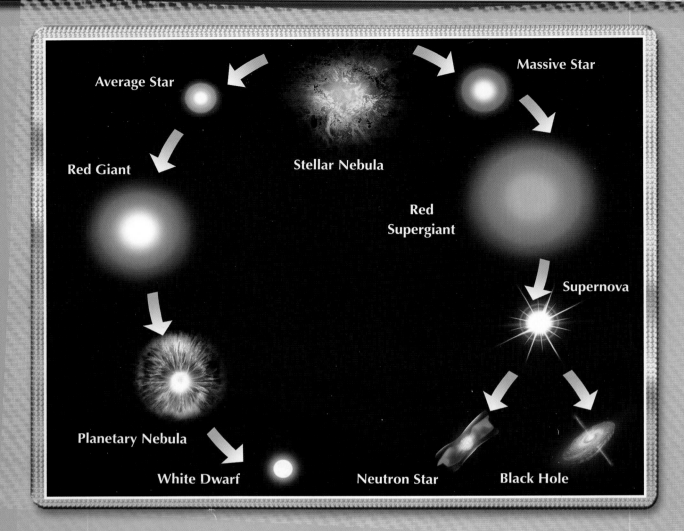

The life cycle of a star depends on its mass, as well as many other factors. This diagram shows three possible life cycles of a star, beginning with the stellar nebula.

Gravity is constantly pushing in on the star, while fusion reactions are constantly pushing out from the star. The star must find an equilibrium, or balance. The pressure of the gases from fusion reactions pushing out must be the same as the pressure of the gravity pushing in. Stars that can reach equilibrium do so quickly. These stars never grow very large.

Each fusion reaction gives off, or radiates, light and gas. Gravity pushes some back into the star. The rest of the light and gas drifts away and cools. It forms the cooler edges of the shell around the core.

Color can tell us about the temperature of a star's surface. Stars that appear red or orange have a cooler surface. Stars that appear blue or white have a hotter surface temperature. What does this tell you about our Sun? Its surface is certainly not the hottest in the galaxy! The Sun appears to be a yellowish orange. That means its surface is warmer than a red star, but cooler than a blue star.

Yet, color only tells the temperature of the star's surface. It holds no clues to the temperature of the core. Suppose the core of one star were cooler than that of another. The atoms in the cooler core would move more slowly and bump into each other less often. This would create fewer fusion reactions. But if the core were superhot, atoms would move faster. They would bump into each other more often, resulting in more fusion reactions. More fusion reactions would make it hard for the star to find equilibrium. The outward pressure of the radiating gases would be strong. It could be greater than the pressure of gravity. During this time the star might look blue.

The temperatures of stars are measured in units called degrees Kelvin. Just how hot is a star? The surface temperature of an average star like our Sun is about 6,000 degrees Kelvin (10,340 degrees Fahrenheit). The core is even hotter. It can reach 14,000 degrees Kelvin (24,750°F)! Still, many stars have temperatures higher than the Sun's. Stars can have cores with temperatures that measure several billion degrees Kelvin!

Our Sun's color tells us that it is warmer than the red giant Betelgeuse, but cooler than a white dwarf.

Betelgeuse   Sun   White dwarf

The Death of Stars

Like all good things, the life of a beautiful star must come to an end.

The death of a star can take different forms. How long a star lives and how it dies usually depend on its mass.

First, let's look at a small to average-sized star, like our Sun. Such stars usually live the longest. Eventually, though, the star runs out of hydrogen for fusion reactions. Its core compacts as gravity pushes it in. The core becomes dense, which means more mass is packed into a smaller space. The squeezing will make the core hotter. To cool the core down, gases will radiate from the star, which will grow hundreds of times larger than it has ever been! Now the surface is farther away from the core than before. That means it is cooler—and will appear red. It is now the type of star known as a **red giant**.

The size of the red giant is misleading, though. In reality, the star is near death. It is running out of the gases it needs for fusion reactions. When the star runs out of hydrogen, it uses helium. Over time, though, the star runs out of all gases that can be used for fusion. The fusion reactions stop. The star creates no more outward pressure. Yet, gravity still creates inward pressure.

Don't be scared, this isn't a giant space eye! It's the planetary nebula from a dying star. If you look closely at the center, you will see a tiny white speck. That's the white dwarf. It will exist long after the gas shells have radiated away.

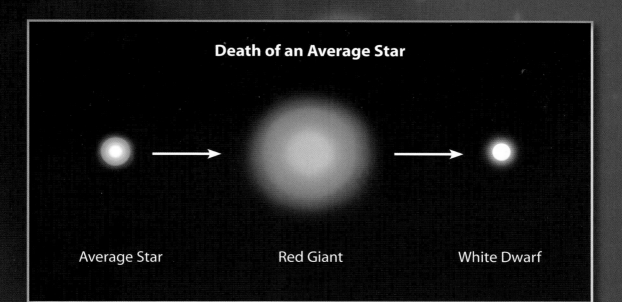

Death of an Average Star

Average Star   Red Giant   White Dwarf

Before it dies, an average star first increases in size. Then it begins to shrink again, eventually becoming a white dwarf.

When the Sun becomes a red giant, it will grow to a hundred times its current size. Unfortunately, it will expand past Earth. Layer by layer, Earth will fry to a crisp. The remains will turn to ash and scatter in space. Don't spend too much time worrying! Scientists estimate that we still have about 5 billion years left!

Now picture a fist crumpling a wad of paper. Gravity acts like that fist. It squashes most of the gases from the red giant back into the core, which becomes even denser. Gases that don't rejoin the core radiate off in a ring of clouds called a **planetary nebula**. The red giant becomes a small, hot star known as a **white dwarf**.

A white dwarf is very dense. It has almost the same mass as the red giant, but takes up a much smaller space. White dwarfs warp space-time. They create deep gravity wells.

Before

After

The large picture shows a galaxy where a red supergiant exploded. You can't see the star in the "before" picture. But in the "after" picture, you can. The star became huge as it exploded. The explosion happened in an instant.

Becoming a white dwarf is the least dramatic way a star can die. A more-massive star can die in a display of beauty. Its journey toward death begins the same way. It begins to run out of hydrogen. Because fusion reactions happen more frequently in a more-massive star, it will run out of hydrogen more quickly than a less-massive star.

As hydrogen runs out, the star will expand into a **red supergiant**. This is the same as a red giant in every way except one: a red supergiant is hundreds of times larger than a red giant. It, too, will eventually run out of helium. The red supergiant will begin using other atoms in its core for fusion reactions. As one kind runs out, the star uses another. As the star uses each different kind of atom, the core grows hotter and hotter. The star compacts into itself. Finally, the red supergiant is nothing but a very dense iron core. Iron can't be used in fusion reactions, so the core stops emitting outward pressure. Gravity compacts the mass of the red supergiant back into the superdense, tiny core that remains.

This is where there is a big difference between what happens to a smaller star and what happens to a larger one. The core of a red supergiant is denser than that of a red giant. The gravity creates stronger pressure. When the core of a red supergiant collapses, the event is very violent. The collapse of the core happens in mere fractions of a second. What is the result? There is a huge explosion known as a supernova!

How huge is the supernova? The force doesn't just turn the solid iron into atoms, it also breaks the atoms into small particles. This is called atomization. After the explosion these particles fall back into the gravity well and combine in different ways. Now, the remaining core has no charge. It is neutral. Thus, these superdense stars are known as **neutron stars**.

How massive are white dwarfs and neutron stars? The white dwarf called Sirius B has an escape velocity of 11,625,120 miles per hour (18,708,817 km/h). That's about 465 times Earth's escape velocity. A neutron star requires even more speed. It has an escape velocity of about 450,000,000 miles per hour (724,204,800 km/h)! That's 18,000 times as fast as Earth's escape velocity! So far, we do not have the technology to travel that quickly. Of course, even if we had, it wouldn't matter. We wouldn't have a chance to land. The gravitational pull of either star would crush us before we landed!

When a supernova explodes, it shoots matter and energy out of its gravity well and into space-time. This creates a beautiful light show. The less-massive matter then falls back into the gravity well. The more-massive matter may escape its pull.

Type I
Stellar Black Holes

It takes the death of a special kind of star to give birth to a black hole. The star must be supermassive.

The third death is the most dramatic by far: the **stellar black hole**. Physicists are not sure just how massive the star must be. Some say it must be five times as massive as our Sun. Others say it must be even more massive than that.

As its life begins to fade, it follows the same path as any massive star: it becomes a red supergiant, and then a neutron star.

But it doesn't stop there. The same process that forms a stellar nebula forms a stellar black hole: accretion. As the star collapses, matter accretes into the point where the core once was, making the stellar black hole denser with every passing second. It stretches space-time further down into a gravity well. In fact, matter continues to spiral into the well forever.

Most supernovas have happened in far-off galaxies. In 1987 astronomers learned of a possible supernova explosion occurring closer to us than ever before—only 168,000 light years away. A light year is a measure of distance that tells how far light travels in one year: 5.88 trillion miles (9.46 trillion km)! So, light from this star takes 168,000 years to reach us. Can you figure out just how many miles away this star is? Astronomers watching it explode were left with a new mystery, instead of answers. Instead of being a red supergiant, the exploding star was blue.

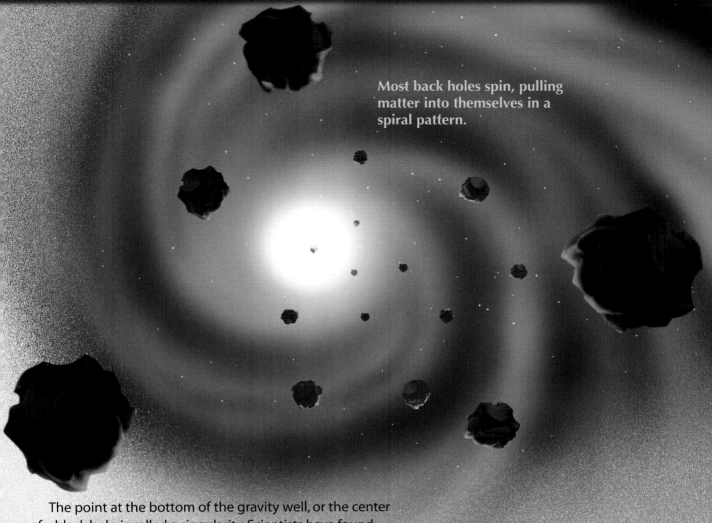

Most back holes spin, pulling matter into themselves in a spiral pattern.

The point at the bottom of the gravity well, or the center of a black hole, is called a singularity. Scientists have found nothing denser. Can anything escape a black hole? It depends on how close you come to the singularity. Its gravitational pull will not be much stronger than the star that collapsed into a neutron star. A massive planet orbiting the star might safely orbit the black hole. If the planet gets closer, that could change. It could then slip into the gravity well, and fall into the singularity. Another danger arises because the black hole becomes more massive by accretion. As it grows, nearby planets can be eased into its gravity well. They are more likely to accidentally venture past the point of no return.

The cycle continues. A black hole grows more massive as it feeds on all the matter around it. The more massive it grows, the more mass it can swallow.

Black holes do not give off any light. It's true that they are invisible. Yet, there are deadly forms of energy radiating from around the black hole. Suppose a nearby planet could survive the pull of a black hole and remain in orbit. Any life on the planet would still die. The deadly radiation would kill it.

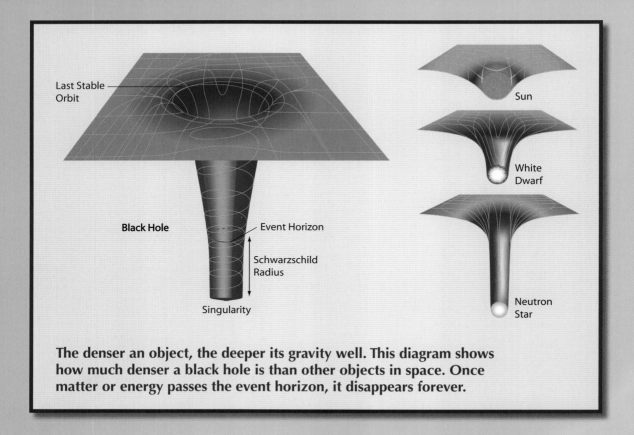

Last Stable Orbit

Sun

Black Hole

Event Horizon

Schwarzschild Radius

White Dwarf

Singularity

Neutron Star

The denser an object, the deeper its gravity well. This diagram shows how much denser a black hole is than other objects in space. Once matter or energy passes the event horizon, it disappears forever.

The singularity is not the only part of a black hole. There is also an event horizon, which is the point of no return. Once an object crosses the event horizon, it is destroyed. The pressure that draws it toward the black hole will tear it to shreds. Only atoms and particles will be left.

This happens to light that enters a black hole. Picture light from a flashlight. It spreads out from its source. If the light had the misfortune to happen upon a black hole, the outside rays might pass by safely. Some other rays would get trapped in a never-ending orbit around the hole. The light waves in the middle would be pulled into the black hole. They would pass the event horizon and disappear.

A black hole is invisible because nothing can escape it. However, as matter nears the event horizon, it becomes hot enough that it gives off energy as light. Scientists can therefore locate black holes by looking for very bright areas surrounding a void of darkness, which is the start of the black hole.

Even though we can't see black holes, we can measure them. Karl Schwarzschild, a German astronomer, wondered how big a black hole could be. He thought that if astronomers found a black hole that was orbiting another star, they could figure out the size and mass of the black hole. Schwarzschild used complicated math formulas that provided very accurate results.

Large black holes have a more massive singularity than small black holes. The distance of space-time between the event horizon and the singularity determines the size of the black hole. Scientists named this distance the Schwarzschild radius. Most people think the size of a black hole should also include the space from the event horizon to the last stable orbit. However, scientists say a black hole begins at the event horizon—where all matter seems to end.

Karl Schwarzschild used math and theories by Newton and Einstein to figure out how to find the size of a black hole.

To better understand the Schwarzschild radius, picture a circle with a point at its center. The point stands for a singularity. The edge of the circle is the event horizon. The radius between them is the Schwarzschild radius. In a black hole, the singularity (the point at the center of the circle) is lower than the event horizon. Astronomers have found black holes whose Schwarzschild radii measure only 6 miles (10 km) long. Others have Schwarzschild radii as large as our solar system!

Deeper into Black Holes

Schwarzschild based his theories on black holes that do not move or spin. This was a problem. Every body observed in space rotates and moves.

A Schwarzschild black hole is one that does not spin. Does it exist? Scientists don't know. It may just be theoretical. A theoretical idea is more concerned with mathematical and scientific possibilities than practicalities. So, a non-spinning black hole could exist according to math and science. Whether or not it exists in reality is a different story. Scientists suspect that all black holes rotate. Bodies that are more massive spin faster than less-massive bodies. Therefore, scientists suspect that black holes spin extremely quickly. In fact, in 1963, a mathematician named Roy P. Kerr used Einstein's General Theory of Relativity to come up with his own math equations. Kerr's equations apply to black holes that can spin and are not electrically charged. Remember that neutron stars have no charge. Kerr's theory on black holes takes that into consideration.

The Kerr black hole, named after Roy P. Kerr, is probably the most common type of black hole.

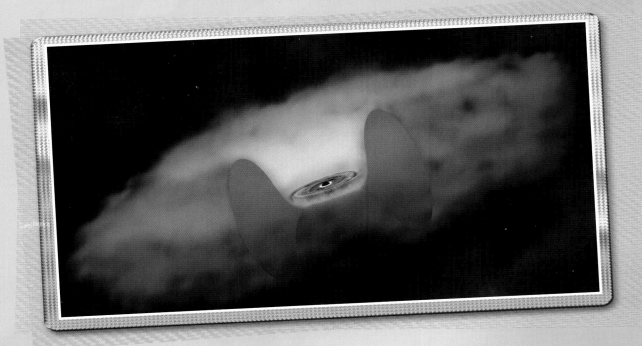

The cloud surrounding this black hole is formed by the debris that is pulled toward the event horizon in a spiral pattern. The black hole draws in matter and energy that is drifting in space.

Theories about different types of black holes abound. One involves a non-spinning black hole that has a positive or negative charge to it. Yet, this is as unlikely as the Schwarzschild black hole. A neutron star occurs before a black hole grows. These rotate extremely fast, and they have no charge. So, Kerr's model is the most likely to occur in space. That's why black holes of this nature are referred to as Kerr black holes.

According to Kerr, space-time around a rotating black hole behaves differently. The energy and mass of the black hole would warp space-time. As a result, Kerr does not describe the singularity as a solid, like a planet. Instead, it is more like a ring that rotates. The event horizon also rotates in the same direction as the singularity. Matter spirals down into the hole instead of falling straight in. As it swirls, it forms a disc, called an accretion disc, of debris and gases around the black hole. This creates a bright glow around the event horizon of the black hole.

Another theory about black holes is that the singularity is neither a ring nor a solid. Instead, the theory is that the black hole is so massive, it actually rips a true hole through space-time! Most scientists agree on one thing: there is no hole in a black hole.

Scientists can only guess how or why these gas jets shoot out of black holes.

Scientists must study the matter around a black hole, since they cannot see the black hole itself. Some noticed that high-speed gas jets were emitted from the general location of black holes. How could this be? Nothing, not even light, can escape a black hole. Yet these black holes seemed to be spewing forth gases with enough force that the jets traveled at nearly the speed of light.

Working with American scientist Kip Thorne, Kerr came up with an explanation. The gases in the accretion disc mixed as they rotated around the hole. Over time, they created a magnetic field between their charged, moving particles. So although it appeared that the jets were coming from beyond the event horizon, they actually came from the accretion disc. Think of making a smoothie in a blender: if you take the top off while the blender is running, most of the liquid will stay inside, but some with get flung onto the ceiling! A black hole is similar. It drags the magnetic field toward the event horizon, creating energy that can launch nearby matter outward.

In 2001 the orbiting X-ray observatory *Chandra* detected X rays being emitted near a suspected black hole. The magnetic field that grows from an accretion disc can get hot enough to give off X rays from just outside the event horizon. By observing these X-ray emissions, scientists can figure out the black hole's mass.

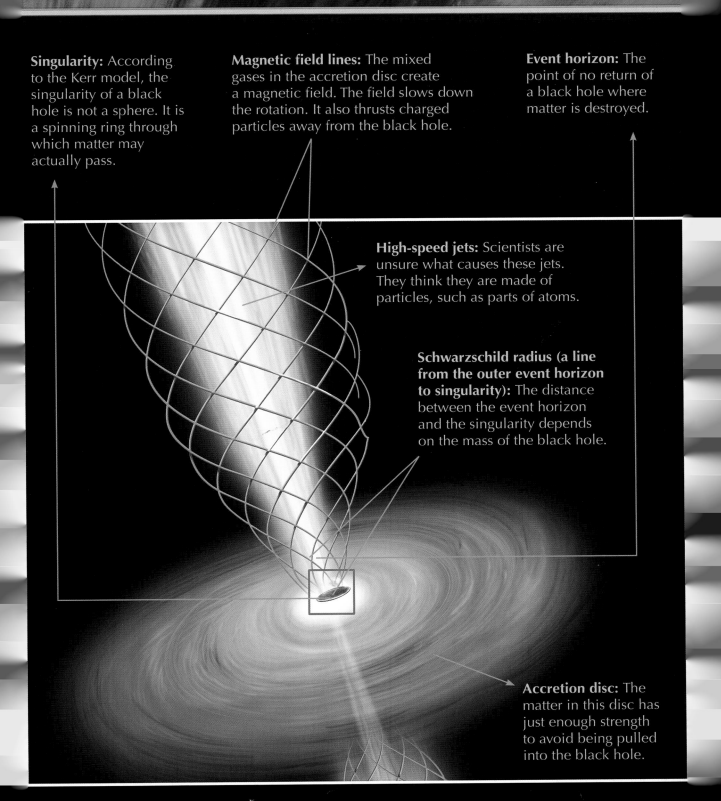

Singularity: According to the Kerr model, the singularity of a black hole is not a sphere. It is a spinning ring through which matter may actually pass.

Magnetic field lines: The mixed gases in the accretion disc create a magnetic field. The field slows down the rotation. It also thrusts charged particles away from the black hole.

Event horizon: The point of no return of a black hole where matter is destroyed.

High-speed jets: Scientists are unsure what causes these jets. They think they are made of particles, such as parts of atoms.

Schwarzschild radius (a line from the outer event horizon to singularity): The distance between the event horizon and the singularity depends on the mass of the black hole.

Accretion disc: The matter in this disc has just enough strength to avoid being pulled into the black hole.

Kerr black hole: According to this model a black hole has no bottom. This has led to several interesting possibilities.

Type II
Supermassive Monsters

Believe it or not, we've discovered something more massive than the stellar black hole. That honor goes to a true beast: the supermassive black hole.

The imagination cannot even conceive their power. These black holes are surrounded by a swirling vortex that creates the **supermassive black hole**. Scientists describe the mass of a black hole in terms of **solar masses**. One solar mass is equal to the mass of the Sun. A stellar black hole may be thirty solar masses. Yet, a supermassive black hole could eat that for breakfast! They have at least 00,000 solar masses! They can have more than 10 billion solar masses!

There are two theories about the formation of supermassive black holes. The first is simple. A stellar black hole continues to take in matter. As it does so, it gains mass. Eventually it becomes a supermassive black hole.

The other method describes a catastrophic event. According to astrophysicists, two black holes could collide and join together to form a huge, supermassive black hole. Two black holes could come close enough together to be within each other's orbit. Matter between the two by them will stretch and squeeze space-time. Over time, the two singularities get closer. Eventually they will fuse together. The moment before they join, energy pushes

Until 2008, the most massive black hole ever located was in a galaxy named NGC 3115. It may have a mass of one billion Suns! Here, you can see a bulge of bright lights made by the stars in NGC 3115. The black hole lurks at the center of this bulge.

and pulls space-time. Ripples of energy are sent out. Theoretically, each time two black holes fuse, they release more energy than all the stars in the universe combined!

Scientists have found that supermassive black holes seem to be at the heart of some galaxies. Because they are so huge, they are not as dense as stellar black holes. Although they have much more mass, their large volume means they have less density. Because of their size, they sit very deep in a gravity well. That means that you would have to be deep into the black hole before reaching the event horizon. If you were massive enough (you're not!), you could dip into a supermassive black hole and live to tell about it. Only a tremendously massive object could resist being pulled past the event horizon.

In 2005 NASA (National Aeronautics and Space Administration) scientists noticed something strange. They had been studying a possible supermassive black hole in the center of the closest galaxy, Andromeda. They noticed a disc orbiting it. The disc was made of blue stars, which are usually the youngest stars. How could stars form in such an environment? The black hole's force should rip any forming matter apart. The discovery led to more questions. This discovery, along with the fact that so many galaxies have a supermassive black hole at the center, made scientists wonder: did supermassive black holes play a role in the birth of the universe?

Scientists believe that when two black holes collide, they can fuse into one supermassive black hole. As they begin to fuse, waves of gravitational force and energy ripple across space-time.

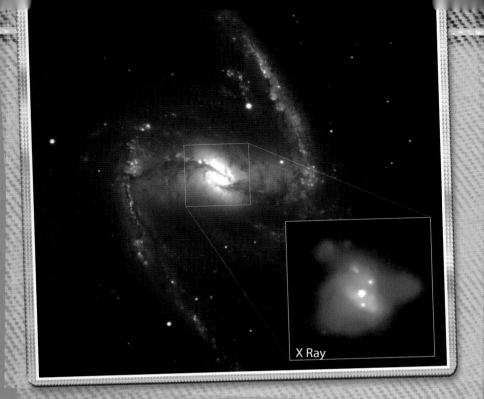

This photo shows the galaxy NGC 1365. The X-ray image (*inset*) shows the black hole and its accretion disc. The eclipse by the cloud enabled scientists to take this picture.

X Ray

The photo on page 26 shows what was once believed to be the most massive black hole ever identified. It is about two billion solar masses. However, in 2008 a new black hole was discovered. It is approximately eighteen billion solar masses! That's as massive as a small galaxy. There may be other supermassive black holes out there that are just as huge, waiting to be discovered.

Another supermassive black hole sits at the center of the galaxy named NGC 1365. Scientists got lucky when a dust cloud passed in front of it, eclipsing energy that normally distorted their view of the black hole. The dust cloud was too massive to be pulled into the black hole. Scientists were able to measure the cloud's size and speed and use that data to deduce the size of the supermassive black hole. Like the Milky Way, NGC 1365 is a spiral galaxy, and the black hole is at the very center. Scientists only knew it was there because they could see light caused by energy radiating away from nearby stars.

What do we know about our own galaxy? Does a black hole sit at its center? Yes! It's named Sgr A* (Sagittarius A-star). It weighs in at about three million solar masses. We're in no danger, however. First, our planet is much too far away to fall into its well anytime soon. Second, it's what is known as a starved black hole. Very little matter remains in its path. It has no source of new energy. In other words, it is not growing right now. Recently, an instrument that can take pictures of X rays of energy caught images of over six X-ray explosions in less than two weeks. The X rays were coming from the accretion disc. Scientists don't know why the explosions occurred.

Ever wonder how these great photos of space are captured when Earth is so far away? NASA can move the camera closer to the subject! NASA has sent many shuttles into orbit around Earth. Some are armed with cameras and telescopes. *Chandra* is an observatory on board a spacecraft. It has an instrument that captures X rays of energy that are invisible to our eyes. Another tool then turns these into images. *Chandra* has been instrumental in finding black holes.

The center of our own galaxy has a supermassive black hole. The red clouds are gases that have been released during explosions.

The Search for the Invisible

Black holes cannot be seen, so how do scientists find them? They look for areas of space-time where time, light, and matter are oddly affected.

It has been proven that mass can warp space-time. If you were near a black hole, particles of light from the same source would reach you at different times. Why? Because the mass of the black hole would warp space-time. This fact is behind an occurrence known as the **Einstein ring**. Scientists can use Einstein rings to find black holes.

Einstein rings get their name because they were predicted by Einstein's General Theory of Relativity. According to his theory, mass can bend energy. Light waves are energy. Gravity and mass skew light waves and bend them, altering their course. This effect is known as the gravitational lens effect.

An Einstein ring looks like a circle of light around a patch of darkness. The pictures to the right show space-time with an Einstein ring. The gravitational lens effect results in light near a black hole being warped. As space-time is pulled into the black hole, each point where light exists twists.

The mass of a black hole causes a dip in space-time. Light waves will scatter as they travel. Some will fall into the gravity well created by the black hole, and others will orbit the well. This combination results in the Einstein ring phenomenon.

Einstein rings are not always visible. In fact, they are found more by chance than by skill. In order to see an Einstein ring, an observer must be directly in front of a black hole or another supermassive object. The light source from another galaxy must be directly behind the black hole. If the observer, the black hole, and the distant galaxy are not in a straight line, the ring will not be visible. Yet, light near the black hole can still appear slightly warped. It may appear flat or streaked.

Space-time with
an Einstein ring

An Einstein ring is a ring of light around a black hole. Light from a galaxy directly behind a black hole is warped. The light rays that are not pulled into the singularity form a ring around the black hole.

In 2008 a camera on the Hubble telescope captured a remarkable image: a double Einstein ring. There is only one possible way this could occur. The spacecraft had to be perfectly aligned with three different galaxies. A black hole or other massive body existed in the first galaxy. The other two galaxies must have been behind that black hole. The two galaxies, the black hole, and the Hubble telescope must have all been perfectly aligned.

This diagram shows what happens if one of the stars in a binary star system becomes a black hole. The new black hole rips material from the other star to feed itself. The heat of the spinning material releases energy as X rays.

In reality, it's difficult to locate anything in space. That's because much of space contains nothing. Scientists can certainly look for black holes by searching for matter being pulled into an object. But there's a much better way. They can look for **binary star systems**.

A binary star system is a pair of stars that orbit the same center of mass. They are actually quite common. Most are two ordinary stars. Yet, suppose one of those stars was a black hole. It would be more massive than the other star in the system. As such, gas and matter from the second star would be drawn into the black hole's gravity well. Slowly, the black hole would suck the life out of the second star. It would draw the star closer and closer.

In 1970, a satellite called *Uhuru* located a huge source of X rays near a known star. They determined that the star, HDE 226 868, was moving as if in orbit. However, it seemed to be orbiting an invisible object. Scientists decided the star was part of a binary star system. The second star was a black hole! Matter from the star sped up as it accreted toward the black hole. Particles bumped into each other as they spiraled toward the event horizon. The bumping released energy in the form of X rays. The *Chandra* observatory can detect these X rays and find suspected black holes.

The gases and dust that make up the star would be depleted. As this was happening, a trail of energy in the form of X rays would appear between the star and the black hole. We have tools to find X rays in space.

A star reaches equilibrium and remains there for most of its life. So even as the black hole was pulling on the star, the star's own gravity would be pulling the star in on itself. This tug-of-war would slow down the star's death. The black hole would pull the outer gassy layers of the star into its well. Then the next layers would be torn off. The black hole would be growing more massive, and the star less massive. Pieces of the star would fall into the hole at an ever-increasing rate. Eventually, the whole star would career into the vortex of the black hole, emitting an explosion of light energy just before it disappeared forever.

In 1970, scientists observed a black hole for the first time. The satellite *Uhuru* captured X rays coming from the accretion disc of the Cygnus X1 black hole. It is a part of a binary star system.

Other Types of Black Holes

Not all black holes are giants. Some scientists have theorized that mini black holes can exist.

A black hole the size of a house would have as much mass as a mountain. So far, these mini black holes exist only in theory. According to popular physics theories, however, there is no reason they cannot exist.

Mini black holes could have a singularity the size of an atom. According to the theory of Hawking radiation, a mini black hole would evaporate very quickly.

Stephen Hawking *(seated)* is one of the greatest minds of our time. He was struck with a disease called ALS (Amyotrophic Lateral Sclerosis), also known as Lou Gehrig's disease, which damaged his nerves. As a result, he has trouble speaking and moving. However, he can communicate through a computer that converts his keystrokes into sounds and words. We owe much of our knowledge of black holes to Hawking.

Quantum physics is a branch of physics that deals with the nature of **subatomic particles**. These are the particles that make up atoms. Quantum physics is sort of the opposite of Einstein's relativity theories. Instead of dealing with the largest scale of matter, it deals with the smallest scale. According to quantum theory, different rules apply to particles this small. They don't follow the laws that we use to explain the rest of matter.

Light waves are studied in quantum physics. They are made of subatomic particles. Quantum theory states that light can change into particle pairs. One particle in each pair has a positive charge and the other has a negative charge. When particle pairs form, the negative particle will fall into a miniature black hole, and the positive particle will escape. To an observer it looks like the black hole shoots out particles. In reality, the particles are escaping as radiation. This radiation is known as Hawking radiation, named after the physicist Stephen Hawking.

As the hole gains negative charges, it loses energy. It also loses mass. Radiation escapes the hole, and the hole grows smaller. As it grows smaller, it releases radiation faster and faster. The vicious cycle results in its death. When it dies, it releases enough energy to cause an explosion.

In 2008 the smallest known black hole was discovered. It has only about 3.8 solar masses, and measures a mere 15 miles (24 km) in diameter. It was found in the constellation Ara within our own Milky Way galaxy.

The Big Bang Theory states that our universe was once a tiny, hot, dense speck that exploded in an instant and then expanded over time. Hawking proposed that as space expanded, millions of mini black holes formed. He called these primordial black holes.

Scientists think the Big Bang happened a little less than 15 billion years ago. According to Hawking, the black holes evaporate slowly. How slowly? Only the smallest primordial holes have died out so far. The larger ones have simply become very small by now—mini black holes. Hawking suggests that the particles radiating from the mini black holes could be almost as old as the universe itself.

It's hard enough to locate supermassive black holes, so no mini black holes have been discovered yet. But scientists are still developing theories on them. Some suspect that they exist in great numbers around the outside of our galaxy. If that is true, and we could locate them, they could teach us a lot about the origins of the universe. During a mini black hole's death, it could possibly emit particles that were 10 to 15 billion years old!

Currently machines called particle accelerators are being used in the hopes of creating a mini black hole. They speed up particles to almost the speed of light, before forcing them to ram into each other. The chances of a mini black hole being made artificially are very small. Even if one were created on Earth, it would not pose a danger. According to Hawking it would die within moments. Earth does not have the necessary environment for it to become stable or grow.

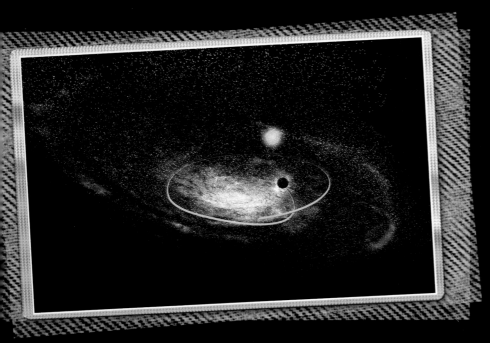

Primordial black holes may still exist, according to Stephen Hawking. In this illustration, yellow rings show where the black holes may be found on the outskirts of our galaxy.

Big Bang

300,000 years after the Big Bang: The dark ages of the universe begin. The universe is filled with energy and matter, in a thick, dark fog.

400 million years: Stars form; mini black holes form from the stars' deaths.

1 billion years: Galaxies begin forming. The dark ages end.

Galaxies evolve

9.2 billion years: Sun, Earth, and solar system have formed

13.7 billion years: Present

How did our universe start? The leading theory is that space expanded from a central point with a huge burst of energy.

Cosmic microwave background radiation was once light from the Big Bang. As space expanded, light moved with it. This light has been traveling for about 15 billion years. Now, it covers the entire universe in an afterglow. WMAP (Wilkinson Microwave Anisotropy Probe) is a NASA satellite studying this energy. NASA hopes to prove that the universe is still expanding, faster than it ever has before.

Time Dilation

A few things about black holes, such as their ability to bend time, make their presence hard to believe.

Einstein predicted that a body could be massive enough to bend space-time and warp it. How could this be? Remember that according to the relativity theories, space and time are part of the same fabric. A black hole stretches space down into its gravity well. This stretches time, slowing it down. This effect of gravity is called **time dilation**.

Time dilation goes against common sense. We like to think of time as moving at the same pace no matter what. These thoughts must be abandoned. Black holes make freaky things happen! A rotating black hole exaggerates the effects on space-time even more. The diagram below shows a theoretical Schwarzschild black hole on the left. Remember that Schwarzschild thought black holes didn't rotate. The diagram on the right shows a Kerr black hole. The grid lines show space and time. Notice how the black hole on the right warps and twists both space and time as they are pulled in.

Suppose that you could enter a black hole and survive. As you entered the black hole, you would begin to fall toward the singularity. As you approached the event horizon, you would follow the same path as space-time. You would also twist and warp with space-time.

A rotating black hole will warp space-time even more than a still one. As space-time sinks under the black hole's mass, it also twists.

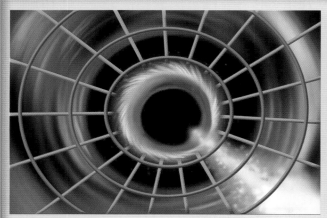
Schwarzschild black hole

Kerr black hole

The closer you get to the event horizon, the more space-time warps. Your body would stretch as you neared the event horizon. If you entered head first, your head would soon be longer than your legs. This is called the **spaghetti effect**. Of course, this is all theoretical. In reality, the pressure of a black hole would kill a person. You would be compressed and torn to shreds. It would not be pleasant!

It's hard to wrap your mind around time dilation. But you can observe it on your own! Place plastic wrap over a hula hoop. The plastic wrap will stand for space-time. Drop a marble in its center. Notice the gravity well its mass makes. The marble represents a black hole. Wrap your fist around the marble from the bottom of the hula hoop. Slowly twist it in one direction several times. Do you see how the space-time twists with it? But a black hole doesn't twist slowly. Twist the marble faster now. How did it affect space-time?

If you could enter a black hole, you would stretch out like a strand of spaghetti before disappearing. This happens to all objects just before the atoms are destroyed.

Time is also affected by the **spaghetti effect**. It is stretched out as it nears the event horizon. A black hole warps space-time and therefore time slows down.

Let's suppose two astronauts are traveling to a black hole. They want to test time dilation. The first astronaut, John, is going to enter the black hole in a safe, uncrushable shuttle. The second astronaut, Suzy, will stay in a shuttle outside the black hole's orbit and observe. If this were to happen, what would each experience?

As John neared the black hole, he would feel as though time were moving normally. Once in the gravity well he would journey closer to the event horizon, with no noticeable changes in time. John would be smart enough to get out before he reached the event horizon. He would report back to Suzy that he was gone two days, and that each day he traveled the same distance. John would be disappointed, because it would appear to him that time dilation was a myth.

Suzy, on the other hand, would have a different view of things. John's first day would seem more like two weeks to her. As he drew closer to the event horizon, space-time would be even more warped. Time would seem to slow even more. To Suzy, John's second day would seem to last about three years! John would have aged two days. Suzy would have aged three years.

Many of Einstein's theories cannot be tested because they require objects with huge amounts of mass—like a black hole. However, time dilation has been proven. An atomic clock is the most accurate type of clock in existence. One was placed on a rocket that orbited Earth. Another was left on the ground. When the rocket returned, the clocks were compared. If time dilation exists, the clock on Earth would show a time slightly ahead. That's because gravity is stronger closer to Earth's center. Sure enough, the clock was just slightly ahead. The time dilation wasn't as extreme as it would be near a black hole. This is because gravity is more extreme in a black hole than on Earth.

Don't be fooled into thinking that a black hole can be a fountain of youth. John didn't stay the same age for three years. He only experienced two days. When he returned to Earth, he would find that he had missed out on several years of his life.

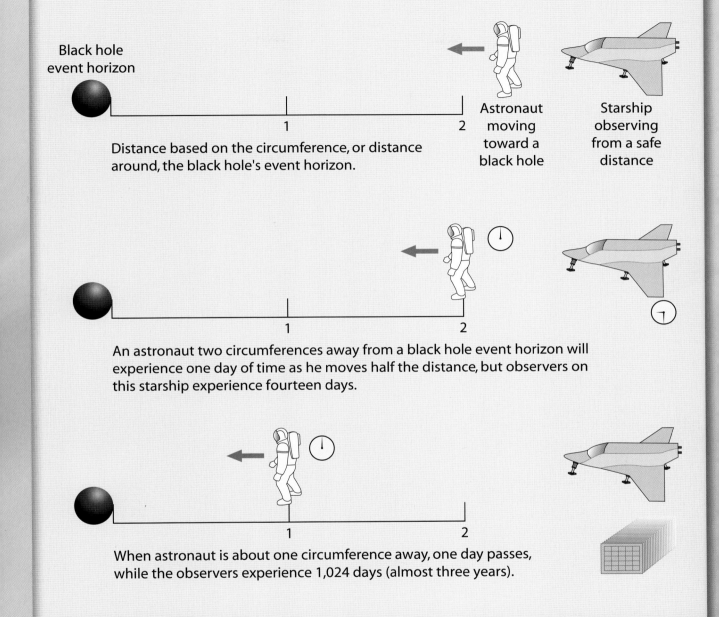

Black hole event horizon

Distance based on the circumference, or distance around, the black hole's event horizon.

Astronaut moving toward a black hole

Starship observing from a safe distance

An astronaut two circumferences away from a black hole event horizon will experience one day of time as he moves half the distance, but observers on this starship experience fourteen days.

When astronaut is about one circumference away, one day passes, while the observers experience 1,024 days (almost three years).

This diagram shows that time is relative, as Einstein proposed. The speed at which time passes depends on a person's location and speed, or their frame of reference.

Myths and Possibilities

In many popular science-fiction stories, characters time travel through a black hole. It's a cool idea, but it's impossible.

Many diagrams of black holes show a hole with two entrances. Some theorize that for every black hole, a white hole, which is the opposite of a black hole, exists. Think of a white hole as an anti–black hole. While a black holes draws in any matter that crosses its event horizon, a white hole ejects, or spits out, matter from its event horizon. White holes are only theoretical, however.

Another well-known idea involves a wormhole. Supposedly, a tunnel exists between a white hole and a black hole. Anything that could survive being crushed in a wormhole would most likely die from intense radiation. However, let's suppose a traveler could survive. Time travel, if possible, would take place when the traveler entered a black hole. He or she would travel through the wormhole, and exit out the other side. The person would be in **hyperspace**, an entirely different space and time. Think of a wormhole as a shortcut in the universe. It would not bring the traveler forward or backward in time.

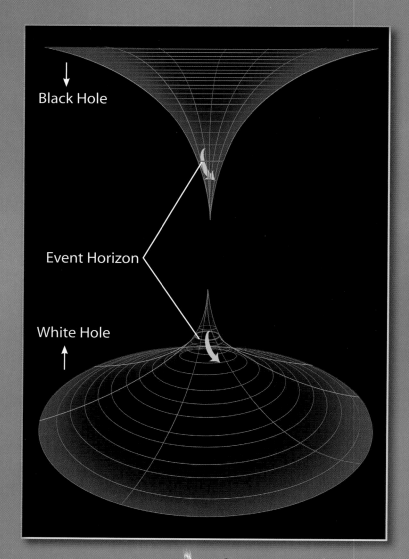

A white hole could never exist. It is purely theoretical. If one did exist, matter could only move in the direction shown by the arrows.

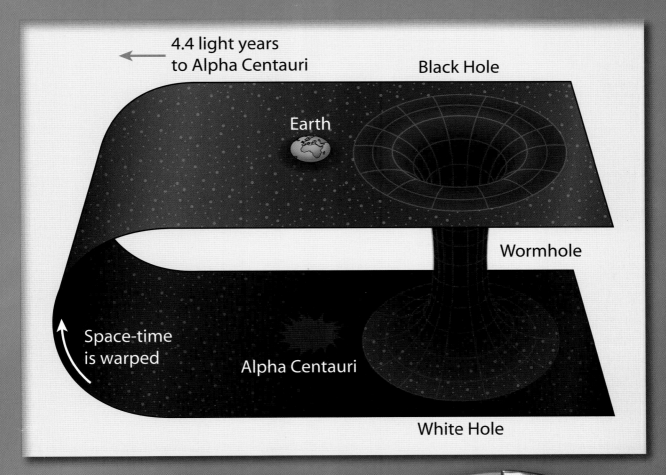

4.4 light years
to Alpha Centauri

Black Hole

Earth

Wormhole

Space-time
is warped

Alpha Centauri

White Hole

A trip to the star Alpha Centauri would take normally 4.4 light years, but through a wormhole it would be immediate!

No one knows where a wormhole traveler would end up. Would it be in an unknown universe? Would it be just a different part of our own? Suppose he or she traveled to a star that was billions of miles away? To the traveler, the trip would seem to have taken a week. In reality, it could have taken thousands of Earth years!

The idea of time traveling through a wormhole fascinates people. Yet, it is more science fiction than science.

There are other problems with time travel. Any action could permanently alter the future. Suppose, for example, a boy traveled back in time and went for a joy ride in a car with the man who would become his father. Suppose they got in a car accident, and his future father died. That would mean the boy had prevented himself from ever being born. So, how could he exist to travel back in time? This paradox, or contradiction, has formed the basis of many movies and stories about time travel.

Could our own galaxy be swallowed up by a supermassive black hole? Sure!

...other movie idea has a black hole sweeping through the galaxies, eating ...rything in its path. It heads straight for the Milky Way. Is this a myth or ...ssibility?

...1961 scientists discovered quasars, which are made of several fused ...rmassive black holes. They are enveloped by a tornado-like vortex of gases. ...ously, a quasar is even more massive than a supermassive black hole. Space-time ...s around it at high speeds, getting hotter with each turn. What is the result? ...ot, swirling gases release energy. The quasar shines brighter than any object ...universe. So where does it get the energy it releases?

...2007 the Hubble telescope photographed the gases and planets of another ...spilling into a nearby quasar. Now astronomers knew the truth. Quasars steal ...nergy from nearby galaxies. As they move through space, quasars pull on ...time. The gravity well around a galaxy stretches toward the quasar, lifting the ...Eventually, the uplifted galaxy will swirl into the pit of the quasar.

...d this happen to our Milky Way? Yes. Should we be looking for quasars before ...out of bed in the morning? No! The light that we can see from quasars is ...s old as the Big Bang. That means a quasar grows very slowly.

In fact, galaxies may actually start as quasars. So be comforted. Even if a quasar came and ate the Milky Way like a candy bar, the matter would eventually give rise to another new galaxy. The supermassive black holes at the heart of some galaxies could even be the remains of quasars. No matter how terrifying black holes may seem, they are not evil beasts. Without black holes our galaxy might not exist.

The Hubble telescope has provided images to prove that quasars get their fuel from snacking on other galaxies.

All quasars are incredibly far away from us, yet they still appear bright. This means they must be very old. The light took a long time to reach us. In 2003 the oldest-known quasar was discovered. It may be about 13 billion years old! This means that light that we see today took 13 billion years to get here.

Glossary

binary star system System where two stars orbit around one common center of mass.

bodies The different kinds of objects that make up the universe, such as planets and moons.

Einstein ring A ring that appears due to light being warped in space-time.

General Theory of Relativity Einstein's theory that states that gravity pulls all objects at the same speed, and that space-time is changed by gravity.

hyperspace Space with more dimensions than the four (three spatial and one time) in space-time.

luminous Emitting light.

neutron star A hot core that remains after a supernova explosion.

planetary nebula A ring of dust and gas given off by a dying star.

red giant A dying star that has run out of hydrogen.

red supergiant A huge red giant that is very bright.

solar masses Way to express mass in astronomy.

spaghetti effect The warping of objects with space-time as they enter a black hole.

Special Theory of Relativity Einstein's theory that states that space and time are not absolute and can change.

stellar black hole A black hole that forms from the death of a star.

subatomic particles The particles that make up an atom.

supermassive black hole A black hole that is much denser than a stellar black hole.

time dilation The slowing of measured time relative to an observer's frame of reference.

white dwarf The remains of a small star that has used up all its fuel.

Find Out More

Books

Jackson, Ellen. *Mysterious Universe: Supernovae, Dark Energy, and Black Holes.* Boston: Houghton Mifflin, 2008. Readers follow a scientist in action as he and his students study supernovae, black holes, and dark energy. Award-winning photography accompanies the text.

Jefferis, David. *Black Holes and Other Bizarre Space Objects.* New York: Crabtree Publishing Company, 2006. Photographs and illustrations accompany the text in this book that explains black holes, the birth and death of stars, and other space phenomena.

Solway, Andrew. *What's Inside a Black Hole? Deep Space Objects And Mysteries.* Chicago: Heinemann, 2006. The text and photographs explain the phenomena of star life cycles, black holes, wormholes, galaxy types, quasars, and the Big Bang.

Websites
http://curious.astro.cornell.edu/blackholes.php
This website details questions and answers from kids to an astronomer regarding black holes. Includes links to the astronomer's favorite sites on black holes.

http://science.howstuffworks.com/black-hole.htm
This website explains the concept of the black holes, including the types of black holes and how scientists detect them.

http://spaceplace.nasa.gov/en/kids/blackhole/index.shtml
This website offers kids activities, instruction, and games related to black holes.

Index

accretion disc, 23–25, 28

Big Bang, 36–37, 44
binary star systems, 32
black hole, 4–10, 17–36, 38–42, 44–45

Chandra, 24, 29, 32

Dolan, Joseph, 5

Einstein ring, 30–31, 36
escape velocity, 7–9, 17
event horizon, 20–21, 23–25, 27, 32,
   38–42

fusion, 10–14, 16

galaxy, 5, 13, 26–28, 31, 35, 44–45
General Theory of Relativity, 8, 22, 30
gravity, 6–19, 27, 30, 32–33, 38–39, 40, 44
gravity well, 8–10, 12, 15, 17–19, 27,
   32, 39, 44

Hawking, Stephen, 34–36
high-speed jets, 25
Hubble telescope, 31, 44–45

Kerr black hole, 22–23, 25, 38, 43
Kerr, Roy P., 22–24

Laplace, Pierre-Simon, 8

magnetic field lines, 25
mass, 6–2, 14, 16, 19, 21, 23, 26–27,
   30–31, 34–35, 38–39, 40–42
mini black hole, 34–36

NASA, 27, 29, 37
neutron star, 17–19, 23

planetary nebula, 14–15

quantum physics, 34–35

red giant, 14–16
red supergiant, 16, 18

Schwarzschild, Karl, 20–21
Schwarzschild radius, 21
singularity, 19–21, 23, 25, 26, 34, 38
space-time, 8–9, 17–18, 21, 23, 26–27,
   30–31, 38–39, 44
spaghetti effect, 39
Special Theory of Relativity, 8
star, 5, 7–9, 21, 23, 26–27, 31–33, 43
stellar black hole, 18, 26–27
stellar nebula, 10–11, 18
Sun, 6, 13, 15, 18
supermassive black hole, 26–29,
   36, 44–45
supernova, 17–18

time dilation, 38–39, 40
time travel, 4, 42–43

white dwarf, 14–17
wormhole, 42–43

X ray, 24, 28–29, 32–33
   Cygnus X1, 33
   NGC 3115, 26
   NGC 1365, 28
   Sagittarius A-star (Sgr A*), 28
   Uhuru, 32, 33